GC2

£7.99

Exile In His Own Country

to Pete
and Gill

Elsng 24/5/13

Graham Calvey

Published by bluechrome publishing 2006

2 4 6 8 10 9 7 5 3 1

First published in Great Britain in 2006 by
bluechrome publishing
PO Box 109,
Portishead, Bristol. BS20 7ZJ

www.bluechrome.co.uk

A CIP catalogue record for this book is available from the
British Library

ISBN 1-904781-94-2

Cover image © Licha Rézeknes, entitled "Harvest", showing his
brother Janis on arrival in the UK, shortly after being released
from the fuel tank of a Sugar Beet lorry.

Exile
In His Own Country

Gareth Calway

Also by Gareth Calway:

Previous Books

"City Zen" (1982)
"Coming Home" (1991)
"Britain's Dreaming" (1998)
"The Merchant of Bristol" (2004)
"The House on the River" (2004)
"Sheer Paltry" (2004)

CDs

"Boudicca: The Anarchy Tour" (1999)
"Marked for Life" (2000)
"Bristol City Ruined My Life But Made My Day" (2001)

Contents

Acknowledgements

DIY was first published in *DIY Today*, *Valley Nocturnes (*as *Newport Nocturnes)* in *New Welsh Review* (- it continues as *The Heavy Metal Sonnets* in *Britain's Dreaming*, 1998)*; Star Teacher* was first published in *School Poetry Review*, *Single to Frome* and *Memorial* in the *New Forest Poetry Society Anthology 2003; Sedgeford October* in *The Rialto*; *The Wash* in the *1993 King's Lynn Festival Souvenir; Valley Frank, Cleavage, After The Show* and *Fall* in *HQ Poetry Quarterly*.

The *Marked For Life* section - along with *Welsh Rugby* - is substantially the text of the touring schooldays show and CD *Marked for Life* and includes poems published in *The Teacher* and by Frontier Publishing. The *Tribes* section includes poems previously published by Bristol City Football Club. The *Harvest* section is taken entirely from previous collections published by King of Hearts Publications and Frontier Publishing and includes poems first published in *Schools Poetry Review*, *Encounter*, *New Delhi London Quarterly* and *New Welsh Review*. *The Ballad of Ashton Gate* was commissioned by Bristol City in September 2004 to celebrate 100 years of the team playing at Ashton Gate and is published for the first time here. The *Petering Out* section includes a poem first published in *The Merchant of Bristol* (The Day Dream Press, 2004).

for Melanie

Foreword

My mother met my father on a train going to Ashton Gate for a Bristol City game in 1954. She was living in Bristol but hailed from Pontypool; he was from Bristol. They had factory jobs but, in their wedding photo, they look like film stars. I was a Severn Beach honeymoon baby, birthed in Usk, Monmouthshire (then a disputed territory) and moving to Bristol shortly afterwards.

My first memory is being attacked by a toucan at Bristol Zoo in 1959. I learned to walk and talk in 1950s Bedminster, to read and write in 1960s Somerset and to cross the teenage wasteland in 1970s South Wales (with only the Methodist Association Youth Club to guide me). Thus my childhood and adolescence are, like Hartley's past, different countries. I revised my O and A levels by candlelight during the miners' strikes of 1972 and 1974, discussing British history in *The Forgehammer* with the men who were making it.

Roy Jenkins, son of the local MP, had lived two doors up. Now he was a Home Secretary inventing the "permissive society". At the age of eighteen I set out to conquer the world and got as far as Guernsey – eight jobs in seven weeks - before beating a Napoleonic gap-year retreat to Weymouth. I then spent five years in the East – at UEA, Norwich. (India came later).

All these places remain branded, like the cows I saw as a boy at Frome market, or coal-like under the skin of the Eastern valley, into my writing. Apart from a UEA poetry magazine, my first poems were published in the mid-80s in School Poetry Association publications and *DIY Today*. The plan was to teach for three years like Auden and then become the world's first Beatle poet. A quarter of a century later, I am teaching English and some remnants of culture (effectively as a foreign language) in a Norfolk comprehensive: am Court Poet at the King of Hearts Centre for People and the Arts in Norwich; Lounge Bard in Residence at the Wolf Brewery and Official Poet Laureate of an underachieving West country football team whose ground is five hours away. I run poetry workshops, judge poetry competitions, review children's fiction for the OUP, write for *Secondary English Magazine* and *NATE News* and, in the tongue of permanent exile (poetry), compose suicide notes from one of the loveliest rural backwaters of Middle England ('Middle' as in *Nel mezzo del cammin di nostra vita*). I tried to give up but it didn't work.

"This coat is torn and frayed.
It's seen much better days
But as long as the guitar plays,
Steal your heart away.
Steal your heart away."

(The Stones, *Exile on Main St*)

Early Doors 1956-1981

Toucan Resistance

I am two.
I am at the zoo.
A toucan's eye
Explodes into 'I'.
His neck's
Giant peck's
A hissing snake
Rippling with hate.
What he don't ave in clout
He makes up in mouf.
Teaches I in my pram
The song of the toucan.

(Bristol Zoo, 1959. Note a toucan's disproportionate beak convinces
other birds that it is a very much larger opponent than it actually is.)

Enclosure

When I was a child (of the 60s),
My father (a child of the 40s) gave me
A palm full of flowerseeds that miraculously grew
Into the picture of blue heaven on the packet.
He toiled meanwhile among his gooseberries
And redcurrants. He was bedding
Down a home, away from the factory
While Mum pressure-cooked, laundered Frome
Town's kit (ten red interlock shirts, one green,
Transforming our line into an apprehension
Of The Enclosure at Bristol City),
Earned shillings from Frome Valley Cleaners
And in between raised me and my sisters.
They had their hand-in-hand pre-school world;
I had the box room painted lavender,
A six feet yard and a shed backed
With stuff I ignited with "safety" matches,
Or watered with my "weeter." I had pet hutches,
A temporary Alps sculpted by the six week
Beatlemania snow of '62-'63 (from which
My toy army never returned.) I had
The rockery it melted back into. I had fruit nets,
Summer country peas, carrots and sticks
And, in the hedge at the top of the garden,
A natural oak stile: *Eden* in smelling distance
Of my blue heaven. Here, outgrowing Little Weed
And Watch With Mother, I played alone
For centuries and ages of mankind's heroes,
Cutting weapons, painting centipedes
(Then trying to save them), battling nettles,
Perpetrating benevolent genocide on ant civilisations,
Came in grizzling when bested by the pus-striped
Bombers my mum called (to rhyme with asps) "wasps",

Smashed the backdoor glass once over the chasing head
Of a mock enemy, a real boy, and one day
Chopped through that fat horizontal crinkly-barked
Oak bough around which all these events were built,
The border and picture frame of my world.

That sturdy barrier (between childhood and bricked in fields)
Was wiped out in an instant. My act was an obscenity
On the lines of patient green-fingered cultivation
That was Dad's enclosure. I tried to hide it, undo
Its disfigurement. I never went near it again.

The Canteens Of Moria

Past bomb-sites into the old hall we'd go
With our escort of teachers, and the smell
Of boiled cabbage as surely served in hell
Would gas the stairwells, pied with potato
Even pig swillers had sent back, and though
The heart - or tongue? - was almost edible
That dread of infant dinners casts a spell
Of vegetable phobia even now.

Watching Moria in "Lord of the Rings"
Decades later in the cinema dark,
I recognise that something in my horror
Of webbed, corrupted, gothic, grave-like things
Was fed to me in infancy; that part
Of what we're forced to eat, we always are.

Dear God, 'elp us to feel ashamed of our bodies...

Dear God,
'elp us to feel ashamed of our bodies.
'elp us to feel ashamed of our minds.
'elp us to feel ashamed of our souls.

Dear God,
'elp us to distrust all political leaders and worldly movements
especially those that *seem* motivated by high ideals
and to put our faith instead into prayer groups.
'elp Gareth to understand that playing cards during prayers
(and writing poems about it for people to laugh at decades later)
means that both he and anyone who laughs is going to hell.

Dear God,
'elp us to accept that we are a waste of time and space
especially when our instincts tell us we're not.
'elp us to distrust all righteous indignation and passion
on behalf of our community or children or family or football
    team or work or dream
as a deceitful snare of the devil.
and to put our trust instead in emptiness.
'elp us to avoid everything that makes us happy.

Dear God,
'elp us to distrust our adult attraction to a grown woman,
'elp us to repress it religiously for so long that we feel brutal
longings for that helpless apple-cheeked angel boy in the choir.
'elp us to feel ashamed of that too, even more devoutly,
but to blame it somehow on the woman.

21

Dear God,
'elp us to feel totally and completely useless,
that human love is a sham, that divine love is beyond us,
'elp us to deny every living moment of our actual experience.
'elp us to feel that we're better off dead.

Dear God, humiliate us.

Frome Sunday School, 1963.

Cooking Up A Revolution

Across the road was where I used to eat
The council shit they served us in the slum
That housed school meals in nineteen sixty one
But here the chef is French, the pommes are *fritte*
And golden waitresses serve smiles and meat
As velvet-dressed as they, pour wine to welcome
This middle aged/class/English gentleman
Whose dad toiled over there in Factory Street.

The Little Bean Book started it, when rice
Emancipated me from lumpen spud
And put the earth-friend, hippy peace in *greens*,
Empowered rebel taste with peppers, spice
And garlic-cheesy student girlfriend quiche
Then Delia's higher course, the food of love.

Frome 04/04/04

1966 *(England 4 Germany W. 2)*

"We won the war- in 1966!"
My Welsh mum beamed in the red-hatted sun,
Commanding me to hoist The Flag upon
Our council pebbledash, porch and privets,
The Somerset exile in which she lived:
And we'd all died, she piped, when that German
Last ditch never-was-a-free-kick spun
Off Cohen's knee and fell to tricksy Fritz.

It was *The Victor's* never ending tale
Of under-doggéd gung-ho Beat-all Brits -
Each Daily written off by Mother's Mail -
Moore, Peters, Hurst, Banks, Stiles, Charlton, Wilson,
Cohen, Hunt, Ball, refashioned as Hendrix,
A mini-short beauty born to die young.

Frome

Welsh Rugby

("they've taken our coal, our iron, our water, our timber...
and we're playing them this afternoon, boys.")

John scores a hero's try
and breaks his collar bone.
It's only a Games Lesson
but it feels like the Grand Slam.
I take his drive for the line
right on the boil on my upper lip.
"Nasty place to have a boil,"
muses Terry Cobner, the Games Master,
Pontypool, Wales, Armageddon,
the Great British Lion who taught me everything
like:
if I come 0.33 seconds late to his lesson,
he hits me so hard on the backside with a Redflash dap,
I can't even cry with the pain.
Last week, Rhys broke his shin failing to make a mark.
I saw the white bone
hanging out of the skin, and the chunks of blood:
one look was enough.
Then up to Ma Kinnock's for 'istory:
leather jacket, hard consonants, Llewellyn the Last and
"Well boys, did you see the match − Cardiff and Arsenal?"
(no 'r' in Cardiff; no coccyx in 'Arsenal.')
The game she saw me break Pike's nose was the proudest day of my life -
but she is as beautiful as the Barley Mountain in spring
and I'm getting to the age when I want to keep my teeth...
I don't want to be Gareth Edwards.
I want to be The Beatles.

Last week, watching 'Terry' hang out of the window
in the middle of another of his recycled RE lessons
yelling at someone on the Rugby field to tackle *even* harder,
I decided it was safer to study Prince Llewellyn
than to re-enact him on the pitch.
I know already that all peoples (even gentle ones)
who've had their sovereignty stolen by a superior force
produce males who all their lives have to prove
it's no reflection on *their* manhoods.

It's difficult for the English to understand this.
It's why Rugby isn't cricket in Wales
but War.

Cleavage

"Therefore shall a man leave his father and mother and cleave to his wife."

You were in the doorway but
I knew you couldn't help me
Even then. In fact your silhouette
Unnerved me strangely, the ghost
Of the Daddy you'd been once,
So strong and secure - and wrong
(It now seemed) about everything.

At 13, I'd found out (for myself)
The hardest of the facts of life:
It ends. Why Death's fingers
Clutched my vitals then is a Mystery
Which discreetly remains
Eternal. I was in a sweat about Hell
When you broke in.

I told you out of dredged up childish
Habit, knowing it would do no good.
You said the right things - said I'd
Get to heaven, was a good boy, "*usually*",
But I disbelieved your word,
Not your judgment, not your virtues,
Not even your love, could save me

Because I was *me*, alone
In the dark with a skeletal hand
Clamping my privates. You closed
The door, following Mum....
You'd gone. The radio scraped
Ephemeral music on the pillow
And I held my doom in my hands alone.

The R.I. Master droned, "See me
After school," set me Bible Questions
(Avoiding Genesis 2:24) but couldn't atone.
Only that girl at the bus stop, whose
New contours muddled the child's coat
I'd torn a *toggle* from the last time
We'd skirmished, made me forget.

Oh not forget, but make it matter less.
Sooner or later, I'd die. But something
That answered in my heart then
Felt like it wouldn't. The darkness lifted
To a decent distance. And life went on
Soon after, though she, shadow-eyed,
Grew aloof and I more awkward.

What good was Grammar and Lit.?
My heart was a cry in the wilderness:
I'd have given all the poems we scanned
For one kiss, her real kiss, that stopped
The longing. You felt the change cleave
Your heart like a blade, but I was *me*,
Lost. And you couldn't find me, Dad.

Pontypool

28

1970 (England 2 Germany W. 3)

"At 2-0 up, my England never lose!"
Swore Dad, and twenty minutes later I
Had lost my father too, wondering why
He'd cheated me like foreign teams, or news
Of English captains nicked, or fools who'd choose
To take wor Bobby off: the Sixties died
In Pontypool exile then, in Groveside
Villas with its Nineteenth Century views.

Pan's People changed to *Legs,* the Oh No band
Yoked John, Starrs fell, Paul's flare stopped making sense,
'uddersfield 'arold became "Hampstead" Heath;
Brazil were back and in the sun they'd tanned
Our English hide, so '66 had meant
Nothing, meant all things pass - except defeats.

Valley Frank

your coaldust
got under my skin
your iron rust
cut deep in the heart of me,
so deep in my teenage heart
that you're never apart from me
tra mor yn fur, I'r bur hoff bau,
o bydded i'r heniath barhau

from *Valley Nocturnes*

1. Seventeen: his own country

The river's prophet tongue I now understand:
I am heir to my druid realm at last.
Girl's curves hover, almost in my grasp,
The boys step back a bit; I have command.
Down Jerusalem Lane, mine's the upper hand,
A Carpenter of Fate in the Christmas
Sun - then the mocking mud, led on by a judas
To his Hotpoint, house, wife, 'friends', looks that brand.

No escape, through a room that madly pulsates
To Pen y Maen bridge, tracing beneath it
Green microdot fields, hills' pie in the sky,
Victorian railings, Dad's Thought Police eye.
I need a real home, away from this place:
A girl, a room, a bed, tavern, music...

2. Made Up

That old religious music plays as I
Get dressed. Clapton now, Madonna later, blues;
I dust my eyelids and sharp glossy shoes
The shade of nightclub nooks and mountain sky
Between the stars, beyond the moon. Meshed thigh
As smooth as Silvikrin, I stand and muse
In drawing where I know I must refuse
A smoky stare, a blushing cheek, a sigh…

This market Magdalene just isn't *me*,
The blackened-station lashes are not mine,
The heightened loveliness is love's disguise;
The chirpy upbeat music isn't happy,
The sweet and fizzy pourings are not Wine.
You want me? Look me in my naked eyes.

Gap Year: Weymouth

The white hot swans of summer
are melting out of the bitter glare
which I, a boy with iced dreams,
held them in.

I spray my eye with Right Guard
and promenade
upon the esplanade.

Bikini'd housewives
are golden beach-babes for a day:
The sand is seen
as pastry with too much margarine.

This girl on my arm
where she's been since October
buttons her pink heart forever away.

I am in a black hole
of this past still-winter

(supplementary benefit spent
on a Romantic education,
Chatterton-teethed heating
soul food, ghost rent)

so very far away from the thing I burn for,
I can almost touch it.

(1975)

Student House

I'm using my own words now
Though I'm sharing a language,
A small self-furnished room in a sprawling mansion
And little sign of a father now
Save for the ash in the chipped chalice saucer
Which might have been his
(It wasn't any of us)
And the bright steamy kitchen
Against the dark garden of apple trees and mystery
Smudging an uncertainty his brow might have worn
And the door-torn carpet, the worn-out walls,
The shabby curtains in the living room
Housing a decay legend tells me went with him.
And the unwashed plates, the serving knife,
Littering last night's supper table,
Hold a nostalgia, cold but not keen, in the dining room
Where we talk and exhale with smoking breath
'Til warmed with the heat of the airing cupboard there
And filled with the incense of cloth aromas,
The room becomes too stuffy and we turn back again
To the hall: the cold, lofty hall with the stained glass windows
Where the telephone on the table and the knob upon the door
Hold no communion with his memory

For if he ever was here seems oddly irrelevant
Knowing now he has gone
And left no address.

(Norwich)

34

Masculine and Feminine Rhymes

A man who killed his father
Was convicted today,
He was hanged by the neck
Till the crime passed away.

A man who killed his mummy
Was convicted by that jury,
He was sent straight to bed
Without his supper, or a story.

1977: A Haunting

Fleetwood Mac are singing of crystal vision;
I'm mourning the death of teenage romance:
A girl, the short term long vacation dance
Of abstract concrete and revolution;
Oil's in crisis: my mind's in sick rotation;
My heart feels nothing of the sudden lance
That smashed its Jericho walls, selling punks
My student sub-let of love's ancient mansion.

Next door, a Shell garage sleeps: I don't, haunted
By absence - hers, mine - the hell-thunder
Of vacuum; chase a ghost through every room,
Armed with a Marxist crit. of Roundhead texts
And a Cavalier prayer on lips struck dumb
By Apocalyptic explosions of doom.

(UEA)

Coming Down

September in Powys: we're coming down
From UEA, the first best friends I've had,
The light of golden years, one going mad,
One going lifelong-AWOL soon, and one –
The girl – post graduation, grown
Dearer than they. Welsh and soft and sad
Autumnal, camped-on mountains, wild, and clad
With mists of valediction, seem to frown

Despite bright skies and open roads, on all
Our interactions. Howard plays guitar,
His face a smoothed torment of discontent,
Best man, sole driver of the grown up car,
Which cracked, crash-bound, passenger Martin stalls
And I make notes on how our friendship's spent.

DIY

'So simple, even a child can do it'
And proof, too, that you're a man
With your toolbox, screws and Tough Exterior.

The simple child within, replete with toys
Is, however, after a morning of broken
Fingernails and dreams, weeping with failure.

Man, a rational animal, resourceful,
Undaunted, silences the child and stares
Once again at Directions to Homo Superior.

Waves of Hobbsian violence, subdued;
An urge to destroy en masse, controlled;
Sublimations of complexes acknowledged as inferior

And the finished Creation stands – pristine – flawed;
Infinitely brighter than the deadwood it replaced
But amateur, improvised, a task for the Inheritor.

(This was the Star Letter in in *DIY Today*, October 1985, and won
me two saws I still use.)

Marked For Life

Star Teacher

Look at the sky, child.
That's Sirius (the Dog),
Orion (the Hunter),
There's the Plough.
That's how, according to our lights,
We know.

Now reach.

Anniversarie for John Donne on St Lucy's Day

I've been watching the fairy bulbs grow into the gloom
Of this Cotswold Christmas city street middle afternoon
And it made me think of you.

Poets are finding it hard to get a place
(I'm chiding late schoolboys) and still see Lucy's face
A dark looking glass through.

It's been a long time since 1631
Since metaphysics met a physics you never knew
But what you didn't do remains undonne.

Gloucester 1981

Marked For Life

Your illegible hand, "Sarah Bitcham, Cardiff University 1932",
Was being formed before my mother was even born.
I came under it in your angry rust sunset,
Your lipstick and powder applied as explosively
As your blistering pen.
Simple sentences were all we were capable of,
You declared, in the accusative. And not a word
We recognised as friendly, or ours,
Or even that brimmed, poet-wise,
Of itself, could we use.
You got your red-hot malice into everything.
Sentenced us to the letter of the language...
Only Mr Lawrence - from his solar
Plexus - and Mr Orwell - from his stubborn
Senses - could liberate us, drunkenly, later
From your three years' regime of cold water
And spiritless pages.

You delighted in Literature as some might in torture.
We were forbidden to write, "I liked the poem
We read by Wordsworth." You'd reduce "I liked" to lashes,
Scald three solid bars across "the poem",
Grill a word as emotive and colloquial as "we"
And with arrows and scrawls that stabbed and blushed
Their brand amid the acne,
Add, in your slap-round-the-face Standard English,
Red-ant stinging the page:
"Simon Lee the Old Huntsman,
By Wordsworth, is an Admirable Poem".
The twenty second time you repeated that lesson,
Our Fifth Year bulks crammed through the legs
Of our Third Year desks,
I stopped writing altogether, could only parrot
Your shrieked corrections.

But you wounded even those;
Usurped 'improved' by 'enhanced' - not because
It was more accurate (it was less) but because
Like that identical lesson on gerunds you gave every
Wednesday afternoon, it proved − as it had for forty years −
How much cleverer you were than us,
How much more incisive you were than the "imbeciles"
Who'd introduced O levels *fifteen* years before; how much
    sharper was
Your Standard tongue than the rest of the Staff's,
The rest of the valley's, fanciful critics, pompous academics and,
    indeed, the whole English speaking world

Except your mother

With whom you still (at 62) lived.

Well, mark this.

Profiles

Mr Hasbeen was one of the Old School
Before it went comprehensive
Who took Early Retirement (at 92)
To avoid the T.V. E. Initiative.
A winter crow Head, ad hoc, ad infinitum,
Shaking chalk mist from bristling lip and gown,
Acrid odour of cigars out-smelling old satchels,
Varnished wood, books, daps and girls' perfume;
Crow-footing down on thirty years' instinct
The corridors he hadn't seen for five.
At 'Prayers' in the Gym, majestically distant,
Sneer-fossiled in close up, with warted cast eye…

The son changed his name to Trendy,
Took a Child Psychology degree
And having 'worked through' his Father complex
Is able at last to love schoolgirls freely.
Now soft dads consult him, in Old School ties
And slow promotion teachers, breeding vague contempt;
Youths, a "waste of space" once, thump in to be "prized",
Ungreyed Heads keep him where old Heads' canes were kept:
Over child-centred junkfood, education's reprocessed,
Over therapeutic feedback, grades 'redefined'.
The rigor of hard-backed old Hasbeen shelved,
The son a new species of nerves – and no spine?

The Driftwood Comprehensive, Dis on Sea poems

1. Parents' Evening

Here we see what the daughters will become:
The puffy and dead-eyed mother
Staring at the father's side, cynical, suspicious,
Demanding where the hell her daughter's

Promise and beauty - which was once hers - has gone,
Even *before* it's in bloom. Typically it's Mummy
Who interrogates, and wonders, against her own
Better judgement and experience, if the *new* New Way

You're peddling is magic after all, and won't all go wrong,
While fathers, bleary from a day's work,
Sit it out grimly, only needled into action
By comments like "he's bottom" or "a berk"

Or not up to it, not capable, not strong,
Or - conversely - agreeing "he has no respect",
Is "dumbly insolent," "ungrateful," "cheeky",
Dumb himself on his daughter...Is her childhood's reject.

2. Mocks

Huddled into football hats and scarves
In their desk terraces,
Stoned on cold and boredom
With fifty two minutes still to go

And nothing left to write about or remember,
Our examinees shuffle and stare
Like a grim crowd at Norwich City
Waiting for a goal that never comes.

In the roof of this breezeblock leisure dome
Propellers flap like aircraft that can't fly.
In one corner, two heaters nibble a glacier.
The floor - a parky one - is marked for badminton

But not for inter-desk ice hockey
As we clatter across it dispensing paper.
And this long siege itself mocks everything - Barbarossa,
Frozen Storage... everything except exams anyway.

3.Exam Invigilation

Today in Norfolk, a boy has *thrown up*
Over Intermediate Science Paper 1 and the era
Of caretakers with buckets arriving within the hour
Is history. The June heat is on and, despite
Open doorways blowing papers like seafront litter
Between deckchair assembly desks, it's beginning
To cook the boy's dinner a second time. And the clock
-A candidate has just informed me - stopped on the hour
Ten minutes *before* I gave them their final time-check:
My shirt has melted from emerald green
To Monsoon purple...

I haven't felt heat like this since Christmas
When, in response to parental complaints
About conditions un-conducive to exam performance,
We hired four blast-heaters from a building site
To roar like rockets in the breezeblock corners
Of our neo-brutalist Sports-cum-Exam Barn
(Put out of commission shortly afterwards
By a Sixth Former trying to drive through it)
Which *still* failed to thaw its December heart of concrete.

Good to recall our cornered wellards though,
Microwaved to a turn, hair frazzle-permed at 100 degrees F,
Dysfunctional faces sedated for the first time in four years...

The rising smell of sick retunes me to the present.
Our caretakers - Godot and Son plc -
Send a memo to say they will arrive a.s.a.p.

-Let's go
-We can't.
-Why not?
-We're waiting for Godot.

It's like trying to make a silk purse out of a haystack,

Like trying to tune a pitchfork in a sow's ear.

4. Ofsted

I am being inspected.
After years of imagining,
little blue-eyed men from Saturn,
they're here!
The one watching me take a register
- noting my hesitation on his clipboard-
looks exactly like Inspector Cluseau.
I feel exactly like Herbert Lom.
He apologises for his trench mac
and tells me he's from Cheshire.
I smile and squeak -
O that's nice
(Cheshire my arse!)
The English Inspector
takes two days to land
by which time I am climbing the walls,
leaping out of my skin every time the door opens,
YELLING at kids for talking
during discussion.
Now *she's* here,
the first day in a purple power suit, the second in puce.
When she talks to me, I can't concentrate.
I am fixated on how flat the end of her nose is,
the flat empty plains on the far side of Saturn,
a planet that invented SATs and the National
Curriculum.

She might not look like
a little blue-eyed Saturnalian
but underneath that approximation
to a human form
lurks a Blimp & Boffin...
     Government...Education...Policy.
Wesley *won't* shut up of course.
He never shuts up.

I thought that this week
that just for once
he would shut up.
I hear myself pleading, wheedling, whingeing,
wielding all the power of fifteen years
teaching syntax, nuance and tone,
"Wes. Wes! there's a bloody Inspector in the room!!
Please. PLEASE. PLEASE!! PLEASE!!!!!
SHUT UP!!!!!!!!!!!!!

5. On Being Locked Inside A Tiny Room By A Well-Meaning Caretaker

I have been locked inside a shrinking room
Alone with my marking, and it's shrinking still.
I have to get out of here before noon.

I must rise and teach a French class very soon
On a cover whose teacher is safely ill.
I have been locked inside a shrinking room.

The caretaker put right (while whistling a tune)
Its gale-clacking doorlatch from hell. Bliss, until
I have to get out of here before noon.

It took weeks to fix, now it's fixed like glue
And he's done it before, with an unlearned skill.
I have been locked inside a shrinking room.

He proved - FROM INSIDE - why the snag can't resume.
"I can't believe you did that. This is surreal.
I have to get out of here before noon."

Now my life bats past my eyelids, my thoughts swoon,
My lungs are shrunk violets, my tongue a spun drill...
I have been locked inside a shrinking room.

I can wait in boiled calm for a saviour to loom
Or waste my breath in screams long and shrill.
I have been locked inside a shrinking room.
I HAVE TO GET OUT OF HERE BEFORE NOON!

6. Healthy Norfolk

"The assembly on healthy Norfolk won't be given this morning
As both members of staff concerned are ill,"
Announces the grave-faced deputy.

I choke down a cough and run past nine hundred kids
Without daring to breathe or meet one eye
Up to the smokers' staff room.

Soon the Monday Morning blues are rocked and ripped apart
By prolonged tear-jerking laughter
And the smokers are feeling better already.

Final Assembly

The unpurged images of term recede
And, hark, the herald angels with dirty faces
Sing in excruciation.
They get younger each year and I,
To serve them half my days resolved,
Get no younger with them.
The praised boy who fishwise leapt with joy
Five Christmas terms ago
Grins at the clapping school now, sardonic.
Where has he gone - are we going - so fast?

O Jesus! still these discordant Years,
That carping torn, that gong-tormented Sea.

Homecomings

In The Bleak Midwinter

watched
by the rich guarded
silence

of cotswold
farms

and a blinding sun
through bare trees

and the jagged saw
of a dog at the gate,

i wonder
what my pilgrimage
to an indian summer
half a world distant
taught me

about this old track
of unchanged england

wrapped up in compliments,
temporary as tinsel,
a feast that goes cold,
a santa that never
really delivers

as i slide

down my frozen hill
of ignorance

on slight city shoes
made in ahmednagar

towards
a painful wisdom.

Cranham, Glos.   Christmas '94

Homecoming: Cardiff

In a morning sunburst, I address the Welsh nation
On the warm and clear-skied Roy Noble programme:
A late and ineffectual compensation
For the publicity *my* show wasn't given!

In the subsequent deluge I perform to eight punters,
Four of them staff, in the Norwegian Church
On the spur of The Bay, and what bardic wonders
Could stop us all feeling so left in the lurch?

But in May night thunder, in the glow of a lamppost
Under old Welsh iron (a low railway bridge),
My lamps picking routes through perpetual roadworks
Where New Wales Assembles, Tiger Bay *lives:*

A dazzling young hooker beams affirmation,
Misreads my kerb crawl from venue to Taff Road
(In frantic lost search of my guest house in Grangetown)
As a punter's – and offers me new Wales for old.

Homecoming: Pontypool

Attending an amateur arts launch out of politeness,
I endure, through a clenched migraine,
The longest speech ever made,

Musing that the Welsh word for précis
Must be
Llanfairpwllgwyngyllgogerychwyndrobbwllllantysilioggochgochgoch,

Applauding the peroration's procrastinated peaking
With mountain-spring heart. Then "It only remains for me
To introduce our *main* speaker for the evening...

From The Welsh

Translations of actual blocks of sentences in a 1970s Welsh learners' book

Peint Mr Juns ydy hwn
This is Mr Jones's pint.
That's new hotel.
The river is very dwrty.
Those are official programmes.
Those are visitors.
Those are not the Barbarians.
Tonight isn't the Big Night.
It isn't the final score.
This isn't a rugby ball....
Is Dai the kicker?
Is Dai the son?
Did he *die* in hospital?
Is the kettle boiling yet?
When does the pub open?
Did she almost win?
Did the child almost drown?
Why did you nearly refuse?
When did she almost die?
The cat didn't die afterwards.
We didn't meet the important man.
He didn't die last year.
She didn't die before Mr Juns.

When did she die?

Return to Egezeter - via Logres

Wherever King Arthur ruled,
This long slow falling through the West
Is definitely where he retreated
And I, who live in the clear East now,
Sense the pull of sodden clay
And the soft mists of dreaming
Whenever I return.
The deep-rooted crime scenes
And green contours of Celtic seeking:
The Chestnut Mares of the Apocalypse;
The Westbury White Horse of the Avatar;
The Hereford cows of munching contentment.
The lush lakes brimming like earthen goblets,
Drizzle-troubled mirrors of empty sky.
Banks of nettles planted by the Romans;
Fields of corn planted by the Druids.
My boyhood overflowing here
In the hot smells of a farmyard,
Like butter from a churn;
My youth across the channel there
The rock bone-close to the surface,
The grass green-blue instead of golden,
The red dragon of winter Gwent
Mirroring the red wyvern of Somerset:
The sum a harvest in the tongue of exile.
Wherever King Arthur ruled,
This long slow falling through the West
Is definitely where he retreated...

Single to Frome

Westbury White Horse appears out of nowhere
As huge as the God of my infancy.
The train bisects a field of wheat and blazing maize
Into a myth of childhood unvisited for 36 years
And I think, "but that's Rodden, where I grew up!"
And an hour later, standing there, it's as if
Some world of ancient legend has come to life.
And *Penny Lane* is playing, as then, council-estate loud
From a house I knew when I belonged here as much
As it still does. Meanwhile, back in 2003,
Mothers with tattooed arms sunbathe in lush gardens
Overlooking skips, cars, internet-addressed vans
I don't remember but also pavements, kerbs
Corners, gateposts, an infrastructure of childhood,
So *eternally* present, in a day so hot, that I wonder
If nothing is real. That face-biting Alsatian still
Haunts his yard of pavement, the Bully still prowls
His wilderness – I see him in every face that looms
Then laugh him off – but they can't hurt me
Anymore. These privets, strawberry plots and fences,
Insider's shortcuts, unconscious Mendip views,
This miniature St. John's Road of what I *lived*,
Was my first map of the world, my first great
Missionary journey in my mother's footsteps
On joy-bent feet. I am alone in another one here:
A riverside pilgrimage in bulky middle age
Through this Summer-set town to a first school
Epic in memory ("The Old School House" now)
Then the hospital - to which my mortal
Injuries once weekly carried me. And a graveyard
Whose small acre, once The Universe, the darkest jungle
Of our games, is now a modest haven from sunstroke
And bustle. Leaving the dead I never noticed

When I ran among these phantom children,
Or posed here in gangs of Secondary Mods
Keeping my Grammar School under my cap,
I walk out, blissed, through a stadium of heroes
(Now a small town park under limitless sky)
To spend a blistering half hour getting lost
In pursuit of the street we went up in the world to,
Alas too briefly. The day is an acid flashback
Through innocence, triggered purely by the glory
Of existence. I am a tourist in my own life.

Gran (1909-2001)

You scribble "Are you married?" I reply,
"You came to my wedding twenty years past
To Melanie? - here's a photograph."
You write "She's very pretty" - and I smile;
You add "Who are you?" and I meet your eye
With "I don't know, do you?" which makes you laugh
And recognise a boy you gave a bath
And bussed to Bristol Zoo in times gone by.

You lived in secrets. Even 'Doris', your name,
Might stop us loving you if it got known.
The truth is, how they did things "Years Ago"
When truth stalked cupboards like a skeleton
Thrust hidden hurt upon you, whom we loved.
The truth, the only thing that lasts, is love.

A Country Life

(for Emma)

A Good Friday

Blood-orange sun lazing down into the sea,
Full moon ghosting up the other side of the sky.
All down the sun-slackened tarmac to the woods,
Finches fleece hedgerows like there's no yesterday
And no tomorrow. Round the graveyard walls
Like over-bred mothers, the fields have ploughed
Through yet another winter, lie back in the sun.
Mozart plays somewhere on a holiday radio,
Notes a tossed incense of joy so *alive*
It is almost beyond living. The sky
Is full of larks and I'm full of Real Ale
And full of myself anyway: it's my birthday.
At the foot of a wall of crumbing stone -
A Victorian relic of ivy and railings -
D-A-D stands over a grave in flowers.
"Look, love, I chuckle, they've left out the E."
This tickles my daughter as much as me
And we splutter until I am out of breath...
I am about to meditate on mutability
When her miniature copy of my hand
Hoists me homeward, impatient, a daffodil chill
On the air. Her face is a tiny March leaf,
Her "snuggle-riding" featherweight on my back
Fresh as the daisy that hasn't quite sprung,
A summer in bud. I'm the finished version.
I guess they'll be carving my dates clear as Spring
On one of these stones eventually (paying
The sextons double because of the chalk)
But all in good time. *Carpe Diem.*
Days like these are worth dying for.

Sedgeford, March 29 1991.

On His Birthday

"You cannot live in the present.
At least, not in Wales." RST

"The rhymer in the long-tongued room
Who tolls his birthday bell
Toils towards the ambush of his wounds." DT

All those years ago, I was in a tatty Welsh classroom
Studying *Poem On His Birthday* by Dylan Thomas
And now here I am in a tatty Norfolk classroom
Teaching *Poem On His Birthday* by Dylan Thomas
(Same textbook, newer edition). I've got nowhere
Very slowly and now the clock on the wall (essentially
The same wall) ticks up thirty nine instead of seventeen
As I fidget and fill in time as artfully as possible -
Subconsciously still waiting for teacher to come.
A big-hearted girl in year 8 has just tidied up
My slagheap of a desk because she "couldn't stand it anymore"
And Caroline next door has crammed my pigeonhole
With a big red balloon and put HAPPY BIRTHDAY
Over the staffroom noticeboard. When I slip home
For lunch, I'll get all my cards, a request to record
My not-so-slim-as-it-used-to-be volume onto tape for America
And the annual rejection from a Welsh publisher.
Then I'll ease on the moccasins Melanie bought me
Which make me feel like a New Man. But I'm not.
I'm an Old Man, a Boy, enjoying his birthday
Up the Mountain, playing truant from everything
With my dog, Tan, running at my heels.

March 29 1995

70

Look, I have come through

I hear a moan - of the earth, but unearthly -
On the other side of the wall.
I creep round, girding my loins from some horror.
"A lamb's having birth!" pipes a child, beckoning.
I join the haggle,
Watch the quiet kindness of humans
As the lamb's bud-horns lock her
In the coffin of her mother's womb,

Watch them wrestling with spindly legs, dashing for aid,
While, irrelevant but insistent,
A turkey courts hens round our shins,
Feathers at full sail, twirling in absurd vanity,
Tattered, matted, red-sore raw and *ugly* beyond belief.

A man returns with a lifeline of coarse string.
A woman helps him coax birth
From the patiently groaning ewe.

The lamb is dead on the hay.
They lay it at the mother's mouth for her to lick.

"Is it all right?" asks someone, stupidly.
I knew it from the start.

...But the lamb stirs.
My heart shouts with the joy of it.
Life!
Stubborn, hopeless, quivering
Life!

Gressenhall, March 1993

After The Show

Lying in a cornfield with you
near the edge of the harvested bit -
but still with plenty of the summer left -

gazing at shooting stars,
wearing stage-clothes and a Union Jack
thin against the long night's sudden cooling,

Lying in a cornfield with you
leaving an us-shaped impression
that will last all summer,

drunk as a kite on *Granny Wouldn't Like It* *
and an after-performance high, discussing
sex (as usual) and stolen horses -

Leaving an impression that will last
when the corn and the stubble
and the ghosts of this long hurt summer have gone,

when the winter corn is sown
in the flint-bared soil,
when the next green June is grown.

Lying in a cornfield with you
talking about love and a lasting commitment
and an ideal company of players

who would live to perform them,
suddenly believing
they're all here with you.

* A real ale brewed from such cornfields as these.

Recollections Of Recent Family Holidays As My Daughter Steps From Childhood

The last time we went west on holiday
From our workaday alarm-clock, flat-out East,
It was late August, like now. Then,
(In Puzzlewood, in the Forest of Dean)
We came upon a great twin-trunked beech
Edged with rose-sunlight in a dark place.
One of the trunks, low down, had a third
That echoed you, sturdy outgrowth
Of your parents' two decade rooted union.
I didn't write this then because it seemed
(a) Hybrisitic (b) too pat and (c) because you'd
Already complained about exposure
(In my poems) in front of your mates.

Now I don't care. There are things too precious
To keep to oneself. Your childhood
Has been like a thread of heaven,
Through all my work and days
And, like this poem, I'm recording it quickly
Before I lose it. These past few nights
Of hip-replacement purgatory
Under rotting canvas on a Welsh mountain
Sloping everywhere (in the general direction
Of Dante's writhing Inferno) at once
Have recalled Puzzlewood all too sharply!
And now, at "half night" as you call 3 am,
We moon out together for a call of Nature
In mountain grass as sweet as Eden
Amid every spook our fears can summise

An inch from the stars of Paradise.

Somewhere in mid-Wales, 1997.

Going Up

You could just say that we were there for you:
In fact, your last exam I sneaked behind
Your desk and checked your answer line by line
As if that school could still find ways to screw
Up your one chance as they'd just failed to do
With your true application and strong mind -
But by this August morning all is fine:
You've made your sunshine 'A's and you are through.

The strain breaks now in tears of harvest home
And though I numb it (drunk in scratchy corn
And staring, supine, at the moon above)
The truth remains – that soon you will be gone
To bright new fields of discourse, campus dawns
Beyond the tug - and give – of parents' love.

Sedgeford October

Somewhere mellow between

the end of the overblown blackberries

and

the start of the harvested leaves

fused flies

on clinical sills

hint at bleached sun

and

in the hedges

thistle winds to come.

To eyes trained on histrionic heights

of Welsh adolescence,

this stubborn serenity,

these mediaeval colours

are

endlessly reassuring:

a great grey blanket billowing unbroken from the North Pole,

wild chords of geese in its folds;

the flinty, dependable noun

behind mists of adjectives.

Fall

This first fallen leaf, grim turd
Of all that March green light and hope,
All that high blue summer it inters,

Does not appal. I'm *glad* it's gone
With all its apprehensions
Of consummation. Let it loose.

Let it all come down.

from *Memorial*

November 11 1996.
Around the village memorial
A local brass band is playing.
The duffle-coated, white-bearded bugle player
Does not really approve
Of "tributes to men who line up
With medals on their uniform chests."
Just at the point where the heart
Should be hanging on the notes,
He jazzes it up,
Turns the Last Post
Into the Temperance Seventy.

I can smell the dead Autumn leaves
On the still air.
More distantly, I smell
A generation of condemned men.

A fallen summer incenses the pavements.

You've opened the door of this flint cottage wide.
It's letting out all the heat
And, like the broken chairs your bulk entails,
It bothers me that this bothers me.
You're standing there with your wife
In the distressed brown leather jacket
You got on the insurance.
Your bullshit face
Is stunned with reverence.
You smoke,
Pause for a long time between puffs.

For an age, it seems that you feel too respectful
Ever to put the cigarette to your lips again
And when you do,
The fact that it's a roll up, like a soldier's,
Make it somehow right.

As so often, I hate
The person I am in your presence.
I'm in the middle of a story

Telling you about the bugle player
When your reverent abstraction
Silences me.

I'm fascinated
By the change in you,
Overcharged, overcharging
Child of the '80s,
From self to love.
I'm thinking
He's an old bollocks

But I love him.

Later you tell me, you were thinking
About your granddad:
"If he hadn't survived the trenches,
I'd have never been born."

It's the most awful thought in your pantheon.

England Win The World Cup
(1966/2003)

November rain and bales of mildewed hay,
The soil a cemetery of summer's yields,
A brief grey day of mud on lanes and fields
And everywhere the fragrance of decay
And on some field ten thousand miles away
The other side of Earth, a gritty heaven builds
That's made of sweat and English dreams, and gilds
An hour to last as long as England may.

And thirty seven years is laid to rest
As I remember an unbroken heart
That Beatled to a drum that couldn't fail
Believing then that Britain was the best
At everything, believing now we're part
Of something greater, striving for the grail.

The Wash

Dirty December
sunset spilled
on the rippling Ouse
like oil.

A factory -its
smoke clouding
the English sky -

And seagulls,
faces like free-fall
angels
screaming on the grey.

from *Norfolk Carol, 1996*

1. Christmas Eve, 3pm

The elements of Christmas -
Fire and ice -
In this tempered Arctic sun
That burns in the trees.
In these pools like skating rinks
Deep and dark and even.
Ice
In the flinty ground
And the bitter Easterly.
Fire
In the solstice sunset
Bleeding the black woods
And its ice-pink afterglow
And its fire-blue areola.
Ice
In the barn-wide rising moon.
Ice
In my soul as I'm turned
To the unlit wings
That cradle and grave
The sunset's light show.
Fire
In my soul
At a rising star
Burning like ice
In the polar blue.

Fire
In my hearth at home
(Crackling through logs),
In the farmer's field
(Roaring through twigs),
Red-raw and orange
Tongues of life-lust:

The vital, stripped down
Simplicities of winter.

3. Christmas Eve 8 pm.

My daughter's dropped the torch
From iced fingers
Snowing the bulb
So the batteries don't connect
To its heart-warming glow
And we can't see the carol sheet...
But the wagon is hung with fairy lights
Frosted with moonshine
And we look like a Christmas card.
And we finally get
Past the too-crowded Inn
To the Promised Place-

A stable of prototypes:

Some faithful sheep farmers
With a vision of angels
If not of the road;

Three love-crazed riders
As seen on Look East
(Come out of the sunset
On secret paths
Across low fields
Of mud-chastened pasture
And shoots of corn the green
'Green' used to be
When the world was young,
Through winter-silent
Norfolk afternoon villages,
Church windows glinting
Like texts of mediaeval Latin)

An unmarried mother
(With a "lily-white"
King Herod of Sleaze
Biting her back,
Her face pure as Venus,
Her faithful Joe
Not quite the winner
Her parents had hoped for)

And tucked out of sight
Behind a bottle bank -
A babe in a crib.
The outlook
None too bright
As I lift our broken lamp
And the brass strikes off
And my voice stumbles in flight
Yet in thy dark streets shineth
The everlasting Light,
The hopes and fears
Of all the years
Are met in thee tonight.

The Music

Life is a bitch, but the songs are great...

In the gloom before work, let the radio play,
Life is a bitch but the songs are great.

The longer I live the more I must say,
Life is a bitch but the songs are great.

Ruin hath taught me to thus ruminate:
Life is a bitch but the songs are great.

Twenty years of schooling merely dictate
Life is a bitch but the songs are great.

Flowers will wither and teeth will decay.
Life is a bitch but the songs are great.

Everything passes; your heart still aches.
Life is a bitch but the songs are great.

You mortgage three decades then death awaits.
Life is a bitch but the songs are great.

You dream siren-holidays: the alarm clock awakes.
Life is a bitch but the songs are great.

You want the Maracana: you get Ashton Gate.
Life is a bitch but the songs are great.

In the name of love, you self-procreate,
Life is a bitch but the songs are great.

A shop-till jingle with words by Yeats,
Life is a bitch but the songs are great.

You lose the plot, like Chandler, like Blake,
Life is a bitch but the songs are great.

The Kylie bird sings and no guitar breaks.
The shit parades, but the *songs* are great.

Saturday ends in a month of Sundays.
Life is a bitch but the songs are great.

I came here for Eden and got Bill Gates.
Life is a bitch but the songs are great.

Life is a bitch but the songs are great.
Let the heartstrings soar, the brass resonate.

The Voice

Sinatra is singing *All The Way* on a foreign radio station,
Across the North Sea and down my snapped aerial.
He's singing from the heart, from the *words*, he means it,
Holding each vowel like a hornplayer,
Phrasing the lyric through the breaks of the song
Like a love-struck shark performing underwater.
I turn it up. And a foreign language is saying he's dead,
Ol' Blue Eyes, is dead - this morning - of a heart attack
And he, even he - never quite gone - won't be coming back.

The Voice, the voice of the little guy, just telling
A story, lives on, though, like a May morning
As it did through all the crackling
Interference of decline: the ghost (impressing
My pillow between Sixties rock) of June
Through even his September years, but *soaring*
On a pungent whiff of Fifties record deck, tossing
Pennies From Heaven to a post-war world
That wanted to dream again. He was my Granddad
In double-breasted suit and Godfather turn-ups
Beaming down on my New Deal mum and dad
On *Songs For Swingin' Lovers*. He was the soundtrack
(Borrowed from Dad along with the suit) at my
Seventies wedding, singing *Love Is Here To Stay*.

The Lean Lark could act, too, outside of the songs,
Natural lines delivered with blazing blue eyes
And finger-snapping aim. A doorman says, *You can't*
Bring that black boy in here.... He's the sax-player
Says Frankie. The doorman sneers, He's a n-
He's my brother says Frankie, with a sweet left hook.
Corny. But true. Like - *There's a lot of people out there, Frank,*
Don't know how to say I love you... You gotta
Say it for 'em. And he does it, so tenderly
(And as lone and rogue-male as a lounge wolf)
It could melt Alaska.

Sinatra is singing *All The Way* on a foreign radio station.
A girl steps through the stalled traffic, naked-
Thighed, soaked to the skin, carrying her shoes,
A gorgeous lithe animal let loose in the city,
Easy and self-possessed as a Sinatra torch-song
Delivered from a bar stool at three in the morning,
It's quarter to three, there's no-one in the place,
Except you and me... sung for Ava Gardner, and all the others.
Or later, tireder, *I have been a rover, I have walked alone,*
Hiked a hundred highways, never found a home
Sung for strangers, in the night, for Farrow, for this girl.

That's you, Frank, because your roving gave it all:
You never found for yourself what your voice hit for *us*
In all that swing, all that swooping caress, all that *jazz*
Loosed from deep in the heart of you, a voice born
Of this roving-spotlit, rat-packed, shot-at century
(Calling you a spick, then a commie, then a gangster):
Born of the blues, of a Jewish violin, of Little Italy.
The nearest to home you got in it was four families
Squabbling over your loot. Well, "Sultan of Swoon",
King of the broken heart-voices who gave their faith
To this world's lost ways, I hope you've found it now.

Frank Sinatra, born Dec 12 1915, died May 15 1998

from *Beatle: a prose poem*

I

Scraping sounds. The repeated hitting of a metallic object: at first without rhythm, then attaining rhythm. A train-rhythmic bell-beat of hard docky places.

- Beat music. Music of the beaten. Only we weren't beaten. We beat. Where are we going fellers?

- To the top, Johnny, to the top.

- And where's that fellers?

- To the toppermost of the poppermost.

- The beat came out of steel and concrete, off wharfs and docksides, out of ships to America, unloaded with the cargoes like the slaves who'd smuggled it in. It came hard-earned out of caverns and warehouses. We quarried the beat from metal and stone.

- We called ourselves the Quarrymen.

- We hammered it into life and shape.

- We called it The Beatles.

The Beat-alls in Hamburg, November 1960. John
Lennon - who is not yet the legend John Lennon - is
leaning against a dockside pillar. He is wearing a shiny
leather jacket and black leather jeans. He looks hard as
nails and sharp as nails but inside he is crying. Paul and
George - teenagers - are in his vision, which is blurred
because it is dark and because he is not wearing his
glasses. Paul is whistling, bouyant as always, even
though a Hamburg sailor's cigarette lighter blacked his
eye on stage last night. The bruise goes with the leather
casing but not the cherub looks. George is too young to
be playing all night concerts on speed. Far too young to
be with that John Lennon but George hero-worships
him. Don't we all? He's a *scream*. Goose-stepping around
the stage Hitler-saluting the Hamburg underworld as
the band rock and writhe and "mach schau" to the
music. Ringo's a star there already, drumming for the
suited resident outfit, Rory Storme and the Hurricanes.
Last summer he was drumming for them at Pwlleli
Butlin's. Not long before that he was at the Dingle
steelworks. When George joins, the Beatles start going
places. Like the Oasis Club, Manchester. When Ringo
joins, they will rock the world. The seagulls are
screeching outside. John is thinking about giving it all
up. It is too hard, too cold. There is too much iron in his
soul, too much iron everywhere. Some of it will kill his
bassist soul mate Stuart Sutcliffe on April 10 1962. Eight
years to the day later, the Beatles will join him. Some
time in between – Sunday December 12 1965 (Sinatra's
50th birthday) they play their last ever live tour date on
British soil, at the Capitol Cinema, Cardiff. Meanwhile
back in the Cavern, John looks at Paul and George. And
Paul and George look at John. They think about it.
Think about it again. They swap their leather jackets for
suit jackets. They comb their Elvis hairdos down into
the Astrid Kircherr fringe. They all beam at each other.

- Yeah!

Will you love me? Truly? Can we live happily ever after,
Cinderella and the Prince? YEAH YEAH YEAH! Girls
girls girls. Diamond-ringed hands. Working it out.
Screaming. Twisting. Shouting. Exploding flash cameras
….

Number One from the start of December until that
magical 1963 snow with BEATLES written in it melted
and the decorations came down three months later.

London, Paris, New York, San Francisco, Sydney….

- Nice feller, Sidney.

A blizzard of camera flashes, freeze flashes of fame.
That Beatlemania grin that lifted a billion hearts.
Conquering the planet, saving the city and getting the
girl.

Everywhere,

For three screaming years.

- Even Cardiff…

II

I've always loved that plucky bastard. Ever since we were boys miming his three cool cat choir, great clunking guitar solos and Cavernous drum from Mam's laundry slats. Raw whoops of joy in four-part harmony.

- The French aren't sure about The Beatles. What do you think of them?

- Oh, we like the Beatles.

- How can you bear teenagers imitating you by wearing Beatle wigs?

- They're not imitating us because we don't wear Beatle wigs…

I cried when the Dave Clark Five toppled them along with the Christmas decorations in 1963 and Mam said it was All Over. When the Fabs were Christmas Number One again in 1964 she said it again. She said it again when they were Christmas Number One in 1965. I thought for an awful moment that when she said it again at Christmas 1966, a Christmas without a Beatles Christmas single after a year without a Beatles British tour, that she was right. When they were Christmas Number One again in 1967, she stopped saying it. She even thought it was them singing *Ob La Di Ob La Da* and *Lily The Pink* as she sang along at Christmas 1968. Well in a way it was. For Christmas 1969, she bought me my first, their last Christmas Number One album. She called it *Happy Road.* I was twelve then and, unlike Father Christmas – and my rebel big sister – they hadn't let me down. They were still here, filling Nowhereland with the soundtrack of luv. It was only when I turned thirteen and needed them most that they split. I was a clinical Beatlemaniac. I needed *Help.* What was I supposed to do in Girl-less bedroom covered with Beatle photos that were my only maps through the teenage wasteland? Try to find The Summer of Love in a Welsh winter without them? Come Together without their Girl? Play *Wings* records?

94

Tribes

England batted all day and won back the Ashes
So a summer ends in harvest, an endless candle flashes.

September 12 2005

The Tribe That Never Was

Blood on the corn
Like poppies, like sails,
Blood on the dawn
In the cornfield of Wales.

A land can't exist
By elegy alone
But now even that 'workshop'
Has been closed down.

"The Celts were invented
In 1700"
(It seems) when Scotland
By England was plundered.

Once Romans slaughtered
The druids of Mon;
Once Cymru's death-foes
Carried it on,

Goddesses, heroes,
Fell from a trance
Into knights and ladies
Of French romance:

Essylte prayed
For a night-black sail;
Boudicca rode,
Gwenhwyfar failed,

And now Mr James'
"Atlantic Celts"
Have finally westered
The westering Welsh.

Blood on the corn
Like poppies, like sails,
Blood on the dawn
In the cornfield of Wales.

It doubtless comforts
The butchered British
Of old to learn
That they never existed.

Myths are carved out
By the hunted killer
But history (it seems)
Is penned by the vicar

In the schoolman English
Of monastery Mon
And the schoolgirl French
That turned us on:

Of Britain's reforging
In the semi-detached flames
Of ironic suburban
Mr James.

Blood on the corn
Like poppies, like sails,
Blood on the dawn
In the cornfield of Wales.

We should be singing
Our bardic song
In seas of corn,
Our voices strong

Of Drustan's truth,
Essylte's love,
Of a black despair
In a sail of dove;

Of Britain's remaking
By the King of May
From the broken sun
Of Boudicca's day;

Of *Arthur, Britain's Making* -
The Arthurian sequel
To *Boudicca, Britain's Dreaming*
And its visionary equal -

Being eagerly composed
While detained all day
By a Person on business
From Norfolk LEA;

Of the red-crests' defeat
By oak-druid seers,
Of King Arthur's reign
For two thousand years...

But in Roma's Mona,
In Angles' sea,
In Blair's middle England
We're history.

Blood on the corn
Like poppies, like sails,
Blood on the dawn
In the cornfield of Wales.

A Jolly Good Friday

Jesus was an Englishman,
The son of Grace (W.G),
Cured ninety nine limbs on the village green
And a leper, before the Last Tea.

Jesus remained a gentleman
Though the crowd's game wasn't cricket,
Carried his cross with stiff upper lip
And was only politely anti-Semitic.

from *Sheer Paltry*

Bard Of Bristol

You're supposed to be at 'ome!!

Standing in my team red before a game, yelling the chants - in and out
   of sync,
The main feeling is of being a complete fraud.
It's not that the team doesn't matter to me:
It matters enough to give me a heart attack.
It's just that, with only distant memories of 2-3-5 to fall back on,
I never really understand what's going on.
There are fifty blokes with a view I could ask from anywhere around
   me
But they each seem to be commentating on a different match.
And I live five hours from Bristol so it's hard to stay in touch.
And, however you market it, the match atmosphere is just like you get
   in a men-only garage -
Oily, reductive, ferociously competitive about everything and nothing-
Aggravated by six pints of booze and ten thousand men-brains,
The kind of thing I went to University to get away from.
If it weren't for the tightening in the stomach every match day,
The inferno of baying noise - purged by love and loyalty
(And comradeship and chantorion and cheer,)
The shiver of the perfectly pitched pass,
The tantalising tactical one twos, the toothsome tingling tackles,
The faith-affirming final ball through the box,
The frantic flash of foot through frenzied ball
The fluent flight of ball through air into flapping net,
The fabulous tapestry of red against blue over green,
The red knights tilting at perfection,
The pavilions of banners, pennants and scarves,
The child's red and white Christmas of the goal consummations -
Then I probably wouldn't bother.

City Win Three Second-Flight Games In A Row

Ahead of and behind
These death-or-glorious victory banners of Logres
Which stretch their dragon red
From Brandon Hill, Bristol,
To Lyonesse in the fabled west

Lie years and decades and centuries of defeat.

This triple crown of defiance
Is but an elfin barque on a black stormy sea,
A flower of chivalry in a fell forest,
A Celtic candle in the Dark Ages
An Arthurian sundown over Somerset...

But how bright those pennants of victory shine!

from *The Beautiful Game*

i. Balls

Football is balls: needs pumped up balls to play
And all the hype comes down at last to balls
And as that US star Reveals Her All
(Well, sponsor-labelled sportsbra anyway)
To breathless world photographers, to say
WE'VE WON THE WOMEN'S FIRST WORLD CUP! it's all
The culture of the male, sharp market stalls
Of bluff and thrust, done derring deals, wha-hae!

But, O, when Stuart Pearce was on the spot
He'd failed to hit in World Cup Italy
(His name in running blood on England's walls)
And flew across the Wembley turf and shot,
A nation's trembling heart in mouth, to see
The world he kicked thump in, what - massive- balls!

ii Away At Cambridge (for Don Calway)

Football is belonging. For me, City,
Bristol City, that boy-sized red and white
I'm donning now for Cambridge, to unite
My aspirations with Adje, Wol. and 'Array
Who don't know me, though clap-happy as Larray
Together when we score, and who would fight
(Though disagreeing) for my native right
To yell bold and sustained inaccuracy.

Football is not belonging. OPPONENTS
In offensively different colours
Kicking, yelling goal for foul, foul for goal;
RIVALS in the *same* colours, exponents
Of the same creed, chanting keep-out dogmas:
One eye, one City, ONE team in Bristol.

iii. Something For The Weekend

Football is sex. When Beckham rammed that
      YEEEEEEEEEEEEEEEEEEEEEEEEES
Down the crowd's throat - having opened his account
With England - (with Campbell about to mount
Him behind) and swivelled his hips like a lech
Because he'd scored with a country, no less,
The earth was moving for us all (the doubts
Stripped off, the World's Cups in our grasp like founts
Of milk and honey) and joined our nakedness.

Sex at its very best, for what is sex
But love, or God, without the permanence,
A crude attempt at ending loneliness?
And what is football but a lonely crowd
Trying to score, a fallen Man, united,
Icarus over the moon and standing proud ?

iv The Beautiful Game

Football is art's reflection of oneness
In a world of divisions; of beauty's truth
Leaping muscle-bound fouls; the dreams of youth
Without its injured ordinariness
Or age's silting of its genius;
The Best without its thickening uncouth
Slurred self-disgrace or bruising disproof
By yobs in boots; the angel dance of studs:

-Like Pele's pass, to gift a certain goal
He'd made his own, to some more mortal bloke
He'd knew *without a call or look* was there;
-Or Maradonna's *second* that turned a whole
Defence, a childhood's poverties, to air
More light than hand of God or head of coke.

Glad To Be A Guy

My daughter loves Thierry Henry
Not only for the same reasons as me.

And when we go away, she brings her brain
And shops for cool clothes on the day of the game

And girls can look great in ways Rooney doesn't
And blokes can be prickly and smell unpleasant

But "Three Lions On The Shirt" always makes me cry
And I know it's all balls but I'm City till I die.

from The Ballad of Ashton Gate

A cement mixer on the Open End
Re-terracing in 'Forty Nine,
Provides a Grandstand View for boys
Like a certain father of mine.

There's a place before the Dolman Stand
Enclosed in 'Fifty Four
Where my parents met and Atyeo scored
And twenty thousand roared

And a flock of swans flew over
The silenced half time crowd,
Their long-craned necks and beating
Wings the only sound.

The old corrugated urinals
A hundred men side by side
Holding their breath and their noses
And finding – like actors – they'd 'dried'.

Watching ageing Stanley Matthews
Out-running City's wing,
So simply crossing it head-wards
City hearts can't help but sing.

Watching Leeds United win
And this without City snarls
At losing to a one man team. Why?
Because the man was John Charles.

Mighty kicks then from Ivor Guy,
Mighty goals from Atyeo,
Gutsy Arnold Rodgers scraps.
These set Ashton hearts aglow.

Gordon Parr under floodlights, bleeding,
Going off without that pen.
Hearts straining last minute winners;
O and *sometimes* getting them!!

Destroyed by Nottingham Forest
A brilliant goal-fixed side,
But seeing Clough's glory at Ashton:
Tempers defeat with pride.

With the '78 'Kop' in our Open End
My father can't hide his bliss...
But the Kop just laughs, says "Fancy
Being beaten by rubbish like this...."

(A miracle repeated at Anfield
Exporting the Ashton roar
When Tinnion unleashed that sweet left foot
In January 'Ninety Four)

Lights going out v Liverpool,
Whitehead's promotion goal,
Stuffing the Rovers – so often (!) -
American Football, and Cole,

Billy Graham, All Blacks Rugby,
Sir Elton John at the Gate;
Darren Barnard's rocket v Bury,
The immortal Ashton Gate Eight.

All the scorers who've made my days
From Bush, Clark to Galley to Lita,
The Atyeo End in excelsis:
No Heaven's gate could be sweeter.

Harvest

There follows a selection from three previous volumes - "Coming Home" (*King of Hearts Publications, 1991*); "Britain's Dreaming" (*Frontier Publishing, 1998*) and "The House on the River" (*King of Hearts, 2004*).

from Coming Home

"Coming Home" is an odyssey and a love story, an
epic of lyrical stages. I imagine a soul journeying
through all the life-forms from gas and mineral through
vegetation, fish, bird and animal up to human. Then
journeying through reincarnation across several millions
of human forms. Then ascending through seven heavens
towards a consummation, a coming to oneself, in an
eternal beloved. Whatever motive force it is that
supports the fledgling as it leaps out of the nest for the
first time is also what dares it to do so, an urge to
realisation. You could call it God, or Love. I borrowed
the spiritual apparatus of this epic from "God Speaks"
by Meher Baba. The mistakes and obstinacies are mine.

from *"Coming Home"*: Evolution

Invocation

The giggle of gas,
The stability of stone,
The mildness and might of metal,
The vigour of vegetation,
The wiliness of the worm
(Out of its depth),
The flowing finesse of a fish
Out of water, beating its scales
Into hard won wings.
The balance of bird
At height of career
Still finding its feet.
The power and the glory
Of the she-tiger
In the cat upon the lap
Thrust from its napping.
The sum of all these
And their greater whole
In human being.

But the growing consciousness
That each is a drop in the ocean
Compared with the love
That drowns life and death.

Of these, muse beloved,
For you,
I sing.

Worm

i'm a creep
a real crawler
no backbone
at all, a

low, humble
grinder, base
mouth full
of soil, a

wet, writhing
hyper-
sensed slave
to all, a

chill, faceless
horror, tight-lipped
toothless
scrawl, a

dim, brainless
shrinker from
harm, a cringing
coil, but a-

live!

and i can turn

To a snake in the grass, or in your bosom,
(Or under a garland of bright apple blossom),
Moving you deep in your bowels:
Subtly developed, sophisticated,
Staring through hooded, lidless eyes
At a dense underworld, dimmed, deaf as Dis,
Feeling my sniff-flicking way with my tongue,
With a wriggle of ribs, swift-scaling the dust,
Dumb, unless rattled, when, breath caught, I hiss.

I'm
Puffed up with sluggish irritation,
Stitched in a dead skin, a splintered vision,
Excreted through rocks like fear, or birth,
Charmed by your writhing arms, scared of sticks,
The dinosaur undead, too potent to handle,
Daemonic, divine, river written in the stars,
Smooth poison keeping Creation sweet,
The dragon. Get off of my back or I'll strike you.

You've wanted me always, under your heel.

Fish

You cleared off
Into Upper Space
Taking your first small giant steps
Into the Primaeval Future
While I stayed,

Coral-jointed a cage
Of nerve-threaded bone,
Fleshing it out with rippling muscle,
Knotting together the deep welling ages
Of fright and flight,

A twitch of my streamlined wings
Keeping me safe,

Shaping up
In the queerest ways
To the all-consuming challenge,
The whelming drowning influence
Of Cold Water,

Coming out of my shell
To conquer the world
With love n warpaint, guts and chainmail,
A show of backbone,
A gritting of teeth

And this rigid fanatic's stare
That never looks forward to anything

Else; head never raised
(Unless I should get
A half-frigid mouth
Hooked on your faithful, singing line)
From a shoalful of furies,

Fears, flirtations,
Fatherly flutters,
A fishy identification with place,
A thirst like an Ocean
I'll never drown:

The unblinking dreams
Of an outgrown brain.

Birth of a Human Being

My snow soul is slowly taking shape,
Falling from heaven to inherit the earth
And the family features of God and ape,
Angel out of my element from birth...
And this is me, this helpless drop of Man,
This perfect mould of bud and mineral,
Crawling, flight, and every earthly thing.
All of it − nothing.
                    Yet I'll assert I AM
In time by striving upright endlessly;
Inherit here a kiss, to milk, like grist,
The love that made me, and by which I'm born;
The word that speaks its perfect mind, the fist
That grasps its imaged God; the whole torn
And bleeding womb of human history.

from *"Coming Home": Ghosts*

England 487

A young Angle on night-watch. The fire goes out.

The fire's flames flee   from dark's dagger drawn,
trees' twigs tremble   my blood runs cold,
death-dread from deeps   from hills, from hollows,
through night-silence numbs   my axe-aching arms...
Now darky-feet drumming   sheep-feet, horse-feet,
wolf-howl, bear-roar,   rain-start and rain-stop;
today's crop of slaves   stir by my lord's boat,
the half-clearing crowds   with ghosts from bad dreams;
no light now but starlight   fierce as gods' faces
to kindle my blood   or make sure my sight:
a witch of a watch   slumped in snake-fern
and no song of heroes   to cheer my chilled cheeks.
When I boast man's beard   I'll bear with my kin
the boat-gorging wave-road's   spite-spitting storms
and go from this fell ground   back to the fatherland.

from *Gwenefore 539 AD*

...Night and this nunnery will fall. Ravens
Will flock on the gore. Let others keep
A glimmer, a glorious page, of Logres alight
Until the dawn. My confession's done.
Still my heart waits for hoofbeats.
(Still, my heart waits for hoofbeats...)

Lady Guinevere (c. 13ᵗʰ century)

Belle ami, si est de nous, ne vous sans moi, ni moi sans vous.

Let them play at boyish games round
A table. Though walled up, bound,
In an unpublished garden, stone
Tower with window, all alone,
This court still revolves around me.
I twist them all round my pretty
Little finger, a studded ring:
The champion knight, the poor king,
Modred, Gawain, my Lancelot.
It's the only power I know.
He comes through enchanted forests,
Rough-horses, haunted castles, mists;
From slaying giants, big bad knights:
Barons with feudal appetites;
Impossible quests for Our Lady,
Sowing wild seeds Love meant for me;
Obsessed so with courtly sin and
Confession – Indulgence's twin;
Greets Artos, old friend – clash of mail
(So grieved his crown still lacks a graal,
So tedious!) He comes to *me*
Who waits… and do not wait to see
The object of his worship pass,
Wasted, into this looking glass,
Wheat-hair, rose-lips, unsown, should he
Choose to deny himself – and me.

I have a heart, self-determined
Core of I Am, God-underpinned,
Won on the Cross, for me. It can
Choose a beloved, a 'husband'
The church would make him. But marriage
On earth's not as it is (a rich
Royal land transaction) as one
With my Lancelot – in heaven.

from *"Coming Home": Involution*

Primadonna and Child

I'm a goddess! But my wild love must come back down to the earth
Just to skivvy for his fixed will, just to suffer a rebirth.

He's my heart's child and I worship every gesture that he makes.
Must I share him with the whole world? Is it tortured with his dearth?

As his cord tugs to that harsh world, makes my heart sore with his cry,
All my wishes free as lightning, wafts of ambrose, know his girth.

From Olympus, love must wing down, past a harp chord in a cloud
Of some cheap scent, past a dream land, to this child's play, to have
        worth.

O Earthed Angel, all your blown heart's sweet enchantment he'll dispel
Crying, "True Love can't be force-fed. It's the breast milk of the
        earth."

Om

In a far land where my thoughts throng by like strangers, I'm at home;
Every dirt track, every silk step over marble, is his own.

There are twinned queues for his rich port, endless pulped forms left to
        fill:
Lovers' thin bribes, like the beggared, seek a short cut to his dome.

Through his doorway, I'm delivered by a rickshaw driven blind
Through his headlights, in his still room, I can think through where
        he's flown.

All unravelled in his presence, all the heavens in a thought;
I am sight-drunk on the soul-bliss of the vision he has shown.

All this heartland made of cracked crags, which his slaves heave up the
        hill,
Every thought-bloom, all this sunlight in my mind's Eye, he has sown.

Were he Lord Ram, though his blood-foe, for his Sita I would die:
Were he Albert, as his Sita, in a grave dress I would moan.

O Miss Know All, distant Empress of the thought world, hear his song:
"Do not seek, child, it's your own veil, like a cobweb must be blown!"

Coming Home

This is God. On the highest of highs through the gulf of a tomb,
(This is God.) I'm on top of the worlds born of mind, spirit, womb.

I am not. Now the bubble has burst, there is nothing but sea:
This is God. I'm as drowned in his kiss as the bud in her bloom.

I'm in Love. All the pain in my heart's disappeared like a dream:
This is God. I am dead to the worlds yet awake to my swoon.

I am him. Now the primal beloved and lover are one:
This is God. I've become who I journeyed towards and from whom.

Oh my love! He's embraced me and brought me at last to himself:
This is God. Now I see there is only myself in the room.

I'm the soul. "There's no dark where there's light, no unknown where
    one knows."
This is God. Little mind has been razed with its search and its gloom.

O my Self! You're beyond the beyond but you're found on the Earth.
This is God, All in All, in the flesh: its perfection, and tomb.

from "*Britain's Dreaming*"

I. Boudicca; Britain's Dreaming

Crowded House are singing
"Julius Caesar
and the Roman Empire
couldn't conquer
the blue sky"
and I think of you, Boudicca,
with that same sense
of singing triumph
even though your glory days
were under grey skies
and short-lived
and weren't innocent
or cornflower pretty
as some Celtic blue summer
and had more to do
with this Norfolk flint
and stubborn soil
than an air of heaven
and even though
Suetonius Paulinus
and the Roman Empire
seized the sunrise
of your three easy wins
as if seizing the flames
of your famous red hair,
and even though
Suetonius Paulinus
and the Roman Empire
crushed your country
if not your body
in his square Roman fist,

sowed harvests of hunger,
rubbed decades of salt
in your people's wounds,
the old word
buddug
still sings in my Welsh blood
in the Norfolk winds
off this unresting sea

buddug
buddig: victory

III Safe European Home

My Muse has been very patient with me,
Waiting demurely for me to turn to her
From dramas of Romano-British women,
Grammar School Muses
(Muses with quads and Latin mottoes)
Vivianes and Guineveres,
Made up women whose woad comes from Paris,
Whose god-lover Llugh translates himself
As "Lancelot Du Lac",
Whose scent isn't animal
Just tested on animals; whose fabulous
Scarlet and sapphire long silk dresses
Are the art that conceals art, the romance
That conceals sex. So naked Boudicca
Turns at last, shakes out her fiery locks,
Lifts me up by my bardic lapels, and says
I am your Muse, and forces her furious lips on mine
And believe me
With that tongue in my throat, that heart in my mouth
Beating out *Boudicca, Boudicca, Boudicca*
I want to sing her dark voodoo warsong
Like it's never been sung before.

Boudicca, Boudicca, Boudicca

I want to ride that chariot with you

Boudicca, Boudicca, Boudicca
in my heart beat,
Boudicca, Boudicca, Boudicca
in my pulse pump,
Boudicca, Boudicca, Boudicca
in my heart punch,
Boudicca, Boudicca, Boudicca
in my pulse thump;
Boudicca
in my blood heat,
Boudicca
in my heart jump,
Boudicca
in my horse feet,
Boudicca .

Death-black, wide-eyes, blood-red dyed hair blown back
horse-brassed ball-smack whip-crack kick-back
bold Boudicca
let the bared breasts ride tonight
cut a chariot dash with a woad-caked ass
lash a sea wind to your thighs

bad Boudicca...

Boudicca, Boudicca, Boudicca,

Boudicca, Boudicca,

Boudicca,

Boud
i
ca
a

I'm kissing the faceless dead ground
On the breast of a Norfolk rise,
Embracing the chill winter grass
With all my body, with all my heart,
And into my mind steps a beautiful maiden
The spirit of some lost Celtic summer
Touching my skin.
Imagine a rowan, her May leaves wet,
Kissing your shoulder with late spring rain,
Imagine your mind like a moistened bud
Drinking her sweetness. Imagine her leaves
Turned light side up with the weight of her berries
August-heavy in the full milk moon.
Imagine her berries
Spilling their juices like healing oils
Over your November loneliness.
Imagine the mother you never had.
That's how Mother Boudicca loves you.

          But what if she's
A death cup, brimming with poison? what
If this bare-armed Bronze Age queen
Is taking me where I've no stomach to go?
I shiver and rise from her poor dead arms
In my raw winter night, hearing soft weeping
Pass on a warm breeze, sense honeyed birdsong,
A deep bronzed arm,
           my pale skin petalled
With flowers from a summer 2,000 years gone...

VII. Choral Ode of Iceni Ghosts

Strophe

We're the restless ghosts in the winds and rains,
Funnelling the valleys, sweeping the plains,
Inlets and warrens that run underground,
Unbridled pathways, unquiet streams,
Haunted hidden corners of rootless sound,
Hives of Iceni, dead and unqueened,
By bronze-breasted redcrests violently weaned,
We're the baby who wails for her dead mother's breast.

Antistrophe

We are dead keening women, whispering grass,
The breath in the lilac and bluebells, the blast
Through the pale yellow oak leaves, hawthorns
And nettles. And that shout, queen of warriors,
From your victory chariot with your triumphant
Horsemen around you! And that salt chill of a winter's
Reprisals that blighted twice twenty summers.
We're the mother who wails for her new baby's death.

Catastrophe

We are the cries in the corn, the harrowings hooted
Under moons of hunger, in the squeals of the hunted,
The creaking of geese through night-forest fears,
The unresting dunes and the moaning wave-break,
We're the memory that's cankered two thousand years
Of Celtic blood with an unhealing ache,
We're the oracles lost in the noise diggers make.
We're the dead daughters wailing for the end of the world.

from The Road to Walsingham

...the chalky green valley slopes
off into heaven. I trace the gentle contours,
the lit, ascetic ash of winter Norfolk,
then light on the flooded stream, water of life
running over in an instant of absolute freedom;
the landscape turns to vision, lightning-flash clear,
fully Earthed, sheep bleating like the bellows of heaven,
the pleasant purl of water on water.

from "Britain's Dreaming": Mountain Ashes

Yellowing Lines

The boy I was at eighteen
Came to me in the night and said
"You have betrayed me..."

You snore by the side of the poem
I scaled the hills for
(Singing names through the mist,

Appalled by echoes),
And in prose without rhythm
Call her "wife",

Delight in nice distinctions
Of colons and semi-colons,
Tense manipulations

Of your subjunctive moods;
Where I wailed for help,
Eyes wide as space,

Raged at Grammar School discourtesies
My head crammed with stars.

WHAT HAVE YOU DONE TO ME?"

Learned to drive
A thickening skin

Past ten a c c e l e r a t i n g years

Where I took my stand

      Deserted

In the rain.

Torfaen Monologues

1

Behind some old shed
Down by the river
I'm tugging at Sian Davies's bra fastener.
"See you again," she'd said,
Her eyes boring *I want you* into mine
So candidly even I believe it.
Now I'm tugging at Sian Davies's bra fastener
And wondering what I'm supposed to do next.
She could tell me. If I ask her.
But I stopped being nakedly honest like that
Since it made me appear the only male virgin in the Year group.
So I'm pretending it's never in doubt.
I listen to the river roaring by
And tug at Sian Davies's bra fastener.
2 decades later I'm a Head of Department
Still pretending I know what I'm doing.
I've been pretending that for thirty years.
What I'm really doing is hiding behind a shed
Down by the river Afon Lwyd
Tugging at Sian Davies's bra fastener.

2

The Boys
  And me
We're off
  Up the Cooler.
Climbing the wastelands
  Brickwork ruins
Slag mountains
  Rusted rolling stock
Summer woods
        Out above the treeline.
I'm tired. It's hot. I'm sunburnt and thirsty.

The Boys pick some berries I've never heard of.
They're all harder than me.
My arm aches from punches.
The Cooler. They keep going on about how great the Cooler is.
It turns out to be a rusted tank of water next to the pit head
        Tasting of pit rust and iron.
Some miners watch us sneaking in.
Their faces are black like bruises.
They look the other way, grinning to themselves.

I pretend to enjoy it,
Dive headfirst into a splashfight.

Tecker picks a scrap so I swing my fist at his temple,
Get blood on my knuckles,
Iron in my soul,
A baptism into coalfield manhood.
Scrap! Scrap! Scrap! Scrap! Scrap! Scrap! Scrap!

3

Gritty steps.
A smell of diesel, tobacco and old carpet seats.
Reminds me of my Old Man.

I wave up at a face in the clouded window. She smiles back,
    vaguely.
She was showing me her milky thighs all the way home.
I was sitting next to her.
I held on tightly to my bus ticket and didn't do anything about it
    as usual.

I call in for the Old Girl's daily bread order.
I hold the loaf out in front of me like a Rugby ball
Run sidestepping down the road as if scoring a try for Wales
Pretending that's what my fantasy is
So that people will like me…

No-one's watching.

God, I hate Rugby.

I hate Rugby.

5.
My Uncle Dai.
Fists broken playing Rugby for the Town team.
Gut swelled with endless pints of *Wind and Piss*.

Every Christmas, a treasure chest of chocs for my mam.
A packet of five cigars for Dad.

Dad doesn't smoke.

I'm fourteen and 'nesh'.
I'm facing Uncle Dai at 'soccer'
On the Bob-a-day rugby pitch
(Levelled from the slag by the unemployed
In those Never Again 30s)
I watch him coming at me.
He's built like a mountain of Pennant grit.

I tap the ball sideways, dance to one side
And leave him standing.

I can beat him.

I can beat the bastard.

6.
My Old Man.
National Service tattooed arms
DEATH OR GLORY.
Face set like mine two decades on.

Redundant.

Three years ago they privatised his industry.
Two years ago they privatised his pension.
They've given him a testimonial.
It says he's indispensable.

We're driving the family to the coast in my car.
It feels funny to be doing it instead of him.

It's hot in Barri.
Chips with everything
Except fish.

All the way home the sun beats down.
Gothic ruins of docks, mines, steelworks.
Slagheaps half-mossed with heather.
Fibreglass windscreens and motorshowroom windows
    dazzling my eye as they catch the sun.

My old man
Anger buried under the shock in his face,
Staring through the windscreen

Not seeing much.

1991

The Conductor

The conductor stubs out
Nostalgia and fag
For the rush down valley
While through his worn bag
Go all the colours of the river,
The green and the silver and the discoloured copper,
Changing
Forever

Coalminer

MCMLXXXIV

Soiled, solid, solitary figure
Working the thin seam of charity
In the main street.

"TRINDER'S ARE SCAB'S"
In red capitals on the disused railway bridge.
Again by the steps up to Tesco's.

I remember you across ten years,
Bar bulging with butties,
Vanguard of the Revolution.

I was a minor then,
Slim student of history,
Sucking the froth of your strike fund.

Now the young push past,
Jobless, to pay a pound more at Style's
For a record they wouldn't look at in Woolworth's.

And the chronically old,
Their health a non profit-making business,
Pass by with a lean look.

And the Griffithstown *crachach* *
The New Inn yuppy:
These are the Crowd now.

I push an old fiver
Into your box.

Futility.

* New - and ungraciously - rich

141

from *"Britain's Dreaming": Sonnets from Hell*

I. You Are Not

To begin at the beginning: you are not -
Some gracious lady with golden hair,
Whose beauty I could trace, or dress, or undress;
 Single: I went half way round the world
To find another poet kneeling in my place
And there are thousands before and behind;
- Alive, let alone here and now with me:
You are not even susceptible to words

And yet I call you and am struggling still
Tongue-tied to please you and to make some sense,
Sure though now I'm not one of your chosen
No matter how infinite your forbearance
Because I speak to the crowd in my heart
Never to the One, the heart itself beating.

II Fever

To have lived once in India is to be
Conscious of the fever behind the plan,
Conscious of the terror behind the calm,
Conscious of the darkness in lit Western cities;
So I've flown out again to your lost century
Disbelieving in switch and tap and fan,
An hygienic, jet-propelled Western Man
Dis-orientated* by your love for me.

Now an Asian fever is taking me places
Which have no painless position to lie.
I escape to my mind but it won't stop
Pitching me backwards through haggling faces,
Eyes and voices, my head in a sweat shop,
Your whole suffering country in my heart's sty.

* "orientated" - literally, *turned to the East*

143

from "*The House on the River*"

The River

In the beginning was the river and the river and the river
And the river dreamed the city but was never the dream
And the river was its mirror but never the reflection
And the river gave it birth but only for an era
And the river was a channel and a conduit for the city
And the river served and cooked, the river fished and gathered,
And the river drained and watered, the river washed and freshened,
And the river was a trade-route and its shore a foundation
For the girl-child on the mudbank and the distant founding father,
For the hunter and the fisher and the merchant and the banker,
For the farmer and the shipman and the grocer and the builder
And the river's liquid softness has a face of blackened flint
For the river is itself and the city is a shadow,
A trumpet-blaring litterer with traffic and lights,
And the river is its alpha and is also its omega,
Its creator and its contrary, the nature of its nurture,
It flows beyond its ending and before its beginning,
It is where the city came from and where it is going.

144

Petering Out

Petering Out

"Surely thou art one of them: for thou art a Galilean, and thy speech agreeth thereto. But he began to curse and swear saying, I know not this man of whom ye speak. And the second time the cock crew. And Peter called to mind the word that Jesus said unto him, Before the cock crow twice, thou shalt deny me thrice. And when he thought thereon, he wept."
Mark 15 71-2.

Nailed upside down at dawn,
The cockerel crowing with the crowd,
I tried to speak up for You,
"Love
 Can turn the world around."

Gravel-voiced but choked
Out of a throat of clay
I threw my rocky word
Too hard, too hard, away.

Now across this sheer water,
A crystal light
Turns and returns
Upon memory's tide.

My father is fishing
Still waters at sunrise.
He turns and winks:
I fear no evil when he is with me.

What voice sounding sure
In the depths of my heart
Drowns the distant breaking
Of a shell's lost cry?

from The Merchant of Bristol

These ships have been my life: The *Mary*
Of *Gloucester*, The *Matthew* and *Peter*
And *Gabriel* of Bristol, The *Christopher*
And *Santa Maria* of Rendry,
The *Thomas* of Portsmouth, *Michael* of Tynby,
The *Nicholas* of Fontraby: whenever
A *Swan* or *Hind* embarks, old voyagers
Set sail once more in mind and memory.

Hispania, my heart is still with you,
Old ships with ghosts of names still bear me there
But leave me hollow-hearted on the quay;
Maria, full of grace, could I renew
The deeds that in my youth I didn't dare,
I'd board a *Mary* now, and seek for thee.

---

* A series of 24 period sonnets inspired by the life of John Smyth, one
of Tudor Bristol's most colourful characters - a merchant, mayor,
city father and large-scale smuggler. "The Merchant of Bristol" must
be the first book I have written about a successful man of the world
rather than in praise of beautiful losers. Smyth was a big player in
Bristol's history during the turbulent years of reformation and
counter-reformation and was the 15th century founder of the Smyths
of Ashton Court. In this final sonnet, he laments the choice he made
in youth to marry for business rather than love.

Meher Baba in Poona 1967

There's an infinite number of ways
To rephrase the maze of your gaze.
Broken face
Unbroken grace
Unspoken.

Your eyes worn again and frayed
Have seen much better todays.
Shrouded sight
Unshrouded light
Unclouded.

On a heart string that never fades,
An unplucked, love-struck phrase
Breaking silence
Unbreaking cadence
Awaking.

The song of my work and days
Aching to blaze your praise.
Toucan nothings
Dumb token mouthings
Unspoken.

* Meher Baba, 1894-1969, spiritual master based near Ahmednagar, India. He observed silence for the last 44 years of his life.